MY WORLD OF DREAMS 2019 - BOOK FOUR

It's February 23, 2019 and I am still at my dad's apartment. His colonoscopy went well yesterday thank God for that. Going to clean his apartment before I leave.

My dream world wow.

About a week or so ago; I dreamt the sea and or, ocean, and I was walking on the sea bed. Meaning, the sea dried up in some areas. I cannot tell you where hence, I have to watch what is going to happen in the Caribbean, North America, the South Pacific, Europe, South America, and Africa when it comes to water.

This morning February 23, 2019 I dreamt Brazil. I dreamt I was in Brazil, **_and children were hungry._** The children were mainly Black, and a mixture of Black. These children never stole anything. As I walked with them, I passed through a market with lots of ripe bananas, pears which is avocado; organic foods. Unfortunately, I was not able to purchase food to give to them, but everywhere you go, children were hungry, and the older generation were disorderly. Meaning, thievery and violence was on their mind from their actions.

So whatever is happening in Brazil, it is going to get worse.

ALTHOUGH I WENT THROUGH A MARKET WITH FOOD, THE FOOD WAS NOT ENOUGH TO FEED THE COUNTRY'S POPULATION.

In my other dream, I dreamt homes, lots of homes that were close together, and painted dark blue. There were no trees because houses were every where, and land space to plant food was scares. People; **_Black People;_** this Black Family was trying to escape to another land. Other people were taking bails of hay; large; very large bails of hay on their back to dam up their homes. They were preparing for disaster.

I do not know which land is going to be devastated by water and or, some disaster. The first family that was escaping was escaping by sea to another land.

2019 wow. Humans have no one to blame but self. We've forgotten that when we sin reckless and rude, sins accumulate – add up.

Sins affect the environment we live in.
Sins affect the life we live.

Sins are a catalyst for death, not just the death of you the person, but of the environment we live in, the earth herself, the death of others, and more.

Evil; wicked and evil people make sure death is fed each and every day. We as humans are the ones to procreate with evil therefore; evil has, and have taken up residence here on earth, and we cannot get rid of it; evil.

Absolutely no human on the face of this earth respect life; God. But then again, not all humans are of God; good and true life.

Different nations; humans have different gods therefore, you have to leave these people alone.

They are not my concern, nor are they God's concern.
Humans live for different reasons.

Some live to kill

MY WORLD OF DREAMS 2019 – BOOK FOUR

Some live to lie
Some live to deceive
Some live to cheat; scam whether financial, or sexual

Some live for money
Some live for greed
Some live to whore – have kids all over the place

Some live to die
Some live to be the slaves of others
Some live to please others
Some live to be controlled

Some live to live

What ever your reason is for being in existence it's and or, is up to you. We all make choices in life, and that choice you made.

Yes, you can say your family made the choice for me.
Your ancestors chose your life for you.

Whatever the choice, you made the choice to live by those choices. So however you die here on earth; you made that choice to die. You did not make the choice to live.

No one can escape death, but that's a lie. Everyone can escape death if they are sinless. If you are not of sin; death cannot touch you. Not even your flesh can die, but unfortunately, no one can live sin free given the sinful environments of earth.

Craps, I forgot, I dreamt Stephen and Damian Marley this morning. Good dream, and I am going to leave things as is because, Damian Marley was eating; no, had vanilla ice cream in a cone in his hand. I told him I am not talking to him because he did not visit me when he was in Canada.

As for Stephen Marley, I think he had a wedding band on his finger. So can't remember.

As for the dream above with the blue houses, I so do not know why my mind is telling me *Iceland.*

Family and people, I truly do not know. Therefore, this warning when it come (s) to the sea and or, ocean, and barricading their homes I am going to extend to all of Europe including Alaska.
Earth is caving in.

Earth is losing her integrity when it comes to the ground. Therefore, ground strength; the ground strength of the earth is not as strong as it used to be.

Like I said, and will forever tell you. **WE AS HUMANS ARE THE ONES TO CAUSE THIS ON SELF.**

WE ARE TO BLAME FOR OUR DESTRUCTION HERE ON EARTH.

WE ARE THE ONES TO BE ERODING THE SOIL OF EARTH.

WE ARE THE ONES TO BE POLLUTING THE WATERWAYS OF LIFE – WATERS OF EARTH.

SEE THAT BOOK – YOUR SO CALLED HOLY BIBLE THAT THE EVIL WHITE RACE HAS AND HAVE GIVEN YOU.

THAT NASTY BOOK YOU PUT OVER LIFE; LOVEY AND OR, GOD.

THAT NASTY BOOK YOU BELIEVE IN.

THAT NASTY BOOK THAT TELL LIES ON GOD; LIES YOU KILL FOR, AND SAY IS TRUE BECAUSE, IT WAS DIVINELY INSPIRED BY GOD.

THAT NASTY BOOK THAT CLASS GOD AS A GIVER BACKER TAKER.

THAT NASTY BOOK THAT PROTRAYS GOD AS A GOD THAT GOES BACK ON HIS, AND HER WORD.

THAT NASTY BOOK THAT SAID GOD GAVE HIS ONLY BEGOTTEN SON TO BE MURDERED; KILLED BY DEATH; DEATH'S PEOPLE FOR YOU THE SINFUL, AND DISGRACEFUL OF EARTH.

Yes there is more. You can thank the writers of that book for lying to you and deceiving you. Lies and deceit that has taken all of humanity to their deaths; hell.

Absolutely no religion can save you because, **GOD DID NOT GIVE RELIGIONS OF MEN; LIARS AND DECEIVERS TO DECEIVE, AND TAKE ANYONE FROM GOD.**

Yes the devil hath time to deceive, and the devil did deceive hence; the **DEVIL CAME AS JEWS.**

INSTEAD OF GOING TO GOD WITH TRUTH AND FOR THE TRUTH, YOU LISTENED TO LIARS AND DECEIVERS AND LET THEM DECEIVE YOU THEREFORE, TAKING YOU TO HELL WITH THEM MORE THAN INFINITELY AND INDEFINITELY, AND MORE THAN FOREVER EVER WITHOUT END.

Now tell me; **IF GOD SO LOVE US; WHY WOULD GOD DECEIVE US?**

IF GOD SO LOVE US; WHY WOULD GOD GO BACK ON HIS WORD?

IF GOD SO LOVE US; WHY WOULD GOD LET THE ENEMY DECEIVE US SO?

You know what let me stop. Yes, I get down on God for loving so, and not loving true, but I know the magnitude of loving so.

Any who, let me stop because I know life, and the cost of the sins of each and every human including mine.

Michelle
February 23, 2019

MY WORLD OF DREAMS 2019 – BOOK FOUR

It's February 24, 2019 and I so do not know why female death has found me.

Do not know why I am dreaming about Beyoncé, and she holding on to me, and vomiting tomatoes.

Family and people; my true family, the dream is so weird because my game play was affecting my dream world all morning.

Things were being eliminated.

I've been playing Best Fiends lately. Fruits of yellow came into play with the dream of Beyoncé, but I am so not worried because; this dream also had to do with children. The dream did not go into detail, and this is all I can tell you. The dream was as I just described. Short.

Like I said, I am not worried about the sell out Blacks of the globe. I know their end, and that end is hell once the spirit shed the flesh. This is their guarantee, hence; I am truly not worried about them. Blacks are going to pay, and pay dearly shortly.

Death must take their children and people home from the different lands globally. Thus, I told you; **NOT ALL OF AFRICA - AFRICANS WILL BE SAVED**, and many Africans should know this. *Many did turn from life - God, and accepted the different god, and gods of men. Thus slavery. Mother Africa had to evict them; the sell out Blacks in her land. Yes, other lands are banned from life in Africa, but Africans will not tell you this. They still live falsely, and have forgotten their true roots and* culture. They too; Africans have been deceiving you the Blacks of the West. The truth of SLAVERY and their, as well as your ancestors are kept secret; hidden from you. See the different religions globally.

What Blacks fail to comprehend is that; whatever is given to death; Satan, you cannot take back here on earth, or in the spiritual realm.

It's not just you who belong to Death; Satan, but your children as well.

Death relinquishes nothing, and this is why A LOT OF BLACKS GLOBALLY ARE BATTERED, AND BRUISED.

We complain about how other nations are unfair to us, but who the hell cares. I certainly don't because, BLACKS KEEP SELLING OUT LIFE; SELF FOR WHAT THE DEVIL AND OR, THE DEVILS CHILDREN, AND PEOPLE OFFER THEM. Therefore, I do not feel sorry for the treatment we as Blacks get globally. We refuse to unite positively and build our own positive community, environment, culture, roots, truth, financial institutions, business, good and true family, and so much more. We are too stiff necked and dunkya.

We've forgotten that WHEN WE RELIQUISH LIFE AND OR, SEVER TIES WITH LIFE; GOD, THE DEVIL AND HIS PEOPLE INCLUDING HER PEOPLE; CAN ENSLAVE YOU, KILL YOU, OPPRESS YOU, HATE

YOU, DESTROY YOU, DO ALL MANNER OF EVIL AGAINST YOU BECAUSE; <u>YOU ARE NO LONGER OF LIFE, BUT OF DEATH.</u>

<u>When you relinquish life, and accept death:</u>

YOU HAVE TO ACCEPT DEATH.
YOU HAVE TO BOW DOWN TO DEATH.

DEATH IS YOUR LORD AND SAVIOUR.

YOU CANNOT BE SPARED THE WRATH OF DEATH.

YOU HAVE TO SELL DEATH.

YOU HAVE TO GIVE YOUR CHILDREN AND OTHERS DEATH. See the many sacrifices; child sacrifices, female sacrifices, male sacrifices, blood sacrifices unto death. <u>The most noted is Jesus of your so-called holy bible.</u>

Now before I continue, I am going to take this further. According to your so-called holy bible, Jesus died on the cross; Cross of Death to save all of humanity. Therefore, since God allowed Jesus to die on a cross; the Cross of Death; that would mean God was Death's bitch because God allowed Death; death's people to crucify his only begotten son. All who believe in this shit that God sacrificed his son to death is saying to God, He God is weak, and death is stronger; more powerful than him; life because, He God had to, and have to bow down to death. You are also telling God he had no balls to stop death, and He God cannot stop Death. Therefore, Death took his only son.

MY WORLD OF DREAMS 2019 – BOOK FOUR

Onwards I go

<u>*When you relinquish life, and accept death:*</u>

YOU ARE DEATH'S BITCH TO DO WHATEVER DEATH WANT (S) TO WITH YOU.

GOD AND OR, LOVEY CANNOT RESCUE YOU BECAUSE, YOU NO LONGER HAVE TIES WITH GOD AND OR, LOVEY.

WHATEVER DEATH TELL YOU TO DO, YOU HAVE TO DO IT. YOU CANNOT REFUSE. IF YOU REFUSE, YOU ARE PERSECUTED AND KILLED. ALL THAT THE DEVIL HAS AND HAVE GIVEN YOU IS TAKEN FROM YOU IN A PUNISHING; MORE THAN PUNISHING WAY.

YOU SIGNED A PACT WITH DEATH THEREFORE, YOUR SOUL AND OR, SPIRIT MUST JOIN DEATH IN HELL. THERE IS NO ESCAPING HELL WHEN YOU HAVE A PACT WITH DEATH.

As Blacks you've forgotten that the job of evil; Death's children was to take you from life. They are locked out of life therefore, if they are locked out, you must be locked out also. And this is what the devil is doing. Just look at the way Blacks disrespect self, sell the devil's agenda, get you; their own people to sin reckless and rude. No, truly look at the condition of Blacks globally and tell me if this; the shit we accept as the truth ordained for us? Now tell me, how can we be better if we truly do not know who we are, and the truth and true truth of who we are?

THEREFORE, KNOW THAT; ABSOLUTELY NO ONE CAN ESCAPE DEATH IF YOUR NAME IS IN THE BOOK OF DEATH. This is why I tell you, know your sins, and know life and death.

Listen, if you have sins on your record, get and or, try to get forgiveness from the person you've erred and or, wronged.

I've told you; <u>NO PRIEST, OR CLERGY MEMBER CAN FORGIVE YOU OF YOUR SINS.</u>

IF A CLERGY MEMBER WHETHER MALE OR FEMALE, PRIEST OR PRIESTESS TELL YOU THAT YOUR SINS ARE FORGIVEN; TELL THEM MICHELLE SAY YOU ARE A BLEEPING LIAR. YES, USE THE F WORD TO THEIR FACE, AND FOR THIS; YOU THE PRIEST, PRIESTESS, DEACON, PASTOR, ELDER ARE CONDEMNED IN HELL BECAUSE; <u>NOT EVEN GOD CAN FORGIVE YOU OF SINS YOU'VE DONE UNTO YOUR FELLOW MAN OR WOMAN.</u>

IF GOD FORGAVE YOU OF SINS NOT DONE UNTO GOD, THEN GOD WOULD BE TAKING THE RIGHT AND RIGHTS OF THE PERSON YOU'VE ERRED, OR WRONGED FROM THEM. Thus making God a dyam liar.

<u>FORGIVENESS CAN ONLY BE GRANTED BY THE PERSON YOU'VE WRONGED.</u> HENCE, THE PERSON CAN ASK YOU FOR A SIN OFFERING IF YOU'VE WRONGED THEM BEFORE THEY FORGIVE YOU.

Yes, this is why many live in turmoil because; *THE CLERGY HAVE THE LOTS OF YOU LOCKED IN HELL. MEANING, YOUR NAME IS IN THE BOOK OF DEATH THUS, THE CLERGY DID THEIR JOB; KEPT YOUR ASS IN HELL BECAUSE, YOUR NAME IS STILL IN THE BOOK OF DEATH FOR THAT SIN. THEY SACRIFICED YOUR ASS TO DEATH; HELL.*

Yes; many of you, including me cannot ask forgiveness for some of our/my sins due to passage of time, lack of knowledge, you can't find the person you've erred, the person may have died. God know this hence, live your life clean. If you are a person that truly like to help others without asking for anything in return, continue to do this. Your good add up, and at the end of the day; ***YOU WANT AND NEED YOUR GOOD TO BE MORE THAN YOUR SINS.***

Also know:

WILLFUL SINS AND KNOWINGLY SINNING, THERE IS ABSOLUTELY NO FORGIVENESS FOR THESE SINS.

Yes, a truthful person that is true to you can save you if they _truly_ love, and care for you.

This I am just finding out.

God's people cannot save you, but if you have a truthful mate, he or she can save you, if you are good and true to them, and they are true, and good to you.

You can save each other; add your goodness and his and or, her goodness together. So yes, all is truly not lost for you in this way.

But, not all is true, and you need to know the sins of your partner. Therefore; know life, and the life you are living.

Like I said, and will forever say; **_IF I AM THE SAVING GRACE OF HUMANITY, I WILL NEVER EVER SAVE ANYONE THAT IS WICKED AND EVIL._** You can kick rocks.

You've hurt others, and I'm to save you? Never ever going to happen. See your hell, and go there literally for real.

Also, **_if you hate BLACK PEOPLE,_** you are going to get the F bomb, or word from me when it comes to extending a saving grace to you. I will not; never ever save you, and trust me, **_I am PETITIONING LOVEY TO NEVER EVER LET ANYONE SENT TO HUMANITY TO SAVE HUMANS TO; NEVER EVER SAVE PEOPLE THAT ARE UNJUST; RACIST DUE TO COLOUR OF SKIN, SEXUAL ORIENTATION, RELIGION, AND MORE._**

Yes, I can hate and despise you, but when it comes to lifting harms against you, I will not do it. I refuse to.

When you instigate hate, I will not have it. Yes, I am racist in some of these books and I tell you, **_but I refuse to tell anyone to go out there and hate you, or even harm you._** It is not right.

F you with your harm and hate. Yes, you can say what you will about me, but I will have the victory over you because, hell will be your domain after I am done.

Lovey is my keep, and I know my protection with Lovey therefore, I worry not about my enemy, and enemies. Nor do I worry about Lovey's enemy, and enemies. **_YOUR APP IS HELL._** And when you are burning worse that a bitch in heat, I will be safely tucked away in Zion with Lovey, and our people happy, and enjoying the beauty, and tranquility of Zion.

Kick rocks. YOU HATE BLACK PEOPLE THEREFORE, NO ONE BLACK, OR ANYONE OF GOD SHOULD SAVE YOUR RACIST ASS. BLEEP YOU. TAKE YOUR DOOMED AND DAMNED; CONDEMNED HELL PASS, AND GO STRAIGHT TO HELL.

God did not tell anyone to hate.

And truly do not come to me with Genesis of your doomed and condemned book – your so called holy bible. God do not put strife between anyone. God is not man; humans that put strife in heart of each other.

Evil do not like good.

EVIL DON'T LIKE BLACK PEOPLE hence; we are hated by every nation/race on earth including some of our own.

Michelle

MY WORLD OF DREAMS 2019 – BOOK FOUR

Please note these dreams are in no particular order. I have so many books going at once that; sometimes I don't know. I truly love to write people. Hopefully I can go away on vacation and get some work done; well finish one particular short story I am working on.

SONGS FOR YOUR LISTENING PLEASURE

FIYAH BUN A WEAK HEART *by the reggae artist Bushman*

TOO MUCH VIOLENCE *by the reggae artist Bushman*

ROBBERY AGGRAVATION *by the reggae artist Bushman*

- ❖ ***WORLD STATE*** *by the reggae artist Bushman – truly listen to the lyrics of World State by Bushman because he is correct. The system we live in is manipulated; therefore, you the citizens of the land have become the confused, manipulated, and controlled. We as Black People need to have our own good, true, positive systems for self and self only. We can no longer build other nations. We have to start building us individually, and collectively.*

WORRIES AND PROBLEM *by the reggae artist Bushman*

DOWNTOWN *by the reggae artist Bushman*

LORD WATCH OVER OUR SHOULDERS *– Garnett Silk*

FIYAH PON ROME *- Anthony B*

NO NIGHT IN ZION *by the reggae artist Luciano*

NEVER GIVE UP MY PRIDE *by the reggae artist Luciano*

❖ ***TRAVELER*** *by the reggae artist Luciano - every nation on earth has, and have taken from Black History. Many say; we weren't there when we were. We created it all hence, all life came from us, and through us. It is only when we as Black People acknowledge, and accept the truth of us then we will see the positive changes in self, and others; other Blacks.* <u>***We have true ROOTS with God,***</u> *and we cannot continue to deny this truth, nor can we continue to teach our children falsely. We are not all cursed, therefore, we have to stop living like, and as the cursed.*

Now on to my dreams.

Michelle

It's a new day Lovey, and my dream world is so strange.

Lovey; why can't Black People unite in goodness, and in truth?

Why are we a part of the left behind?

Why do we kill each other so, and not support each other in a positive, and true way?

Why do we bring down each other so?

Lovey, I truly need to talk to you my way because; the mind can be so sinful, and dark.

We so need to talk about sex, and why our thoughts; well mine can be so sinful and dark; lustful and maddening sexually.

Lovey, why is sexual pleasure in the mind so powerful, and dark?

Why is your thoughts so powerful, and negative sexually?

Why does sex, our sexual thoughts so powerful that it takes hold of you, and get you to do negative things?

Now Lovey, can sex be separated from the body and spirit, and we live a healthy, true, and clean life?

Why is sexual energy so strong Lovey, and why is this energy connected to our body, mind, and spirit?

Why give us such a strong force that we cannot control, or tame Lovey?

Absolutely no one can control their sexual desires and thoughts when that energy comes full throttle and or, throttle Lovey; why?

Now tell me, is sex a sin?

Is sex, sexual pleasure, sexual thoughts against true, and good life?

Lovey, can physical and spiritual life do without sex, sexual pleasure, sexual thoughts?

Can we be cleansed of this force due to negative thoughts; will?

Michelle
September 17, 2018

Dream wise, I dreamt this tall white guy. I say White, but he could be of Middle Eastern descent - White Middle Eastern.

Black hair I believe. No, dark hair.

He had tattoos on his chest. Think pin tattoos.

He was in an ancient boat. Think long boat that have paddles, and could fly.

I wish I could refer you to a movie that had flying boats and or, ships for you to see what I am talking about.

The front of the boat had an animal outlined on it. I can't remember if it's a dragon, but an animal of that effect.

He had a route; travel route outlined. The route was Istanbul, then Iran, then Saudi Arabia. That was his route, and I woke up ; well felt I needed to pee.

<u>I will not analyze this dream because; I truly do not know what flying ships, or boats of old represent.</u>

Babylon, and the children of Babylon is truly not my concern.

Like I say, and will forever say; **<u>LIFE IS TRULY NOT DEATH.</u>**

Therefore; how death's children fight, and kill themselves is truly up to them.

This is going to sound cold but; ***GOOD RIDDENS.***

Life cannot kill, and if humans truly respected life and God; they would not kill each other, or create conflict with each other, or one another.
Yes, I know I will not be like globally for these books; words, but that concerns me not.

Michelle
February 15, 2019

MY WORLD OF DREAMS 2019 – BOOK FOUR

It's February 15, 2019, and the set up is real for my family.

Someone is setting up my son, but I cannot tell you who because; the face of the person is not being revealed to me.

Shit of crap is happening in my family people hence jealousy is a hell of a thing.

But I leave these people and or, this person to time and Lovey.

You hurt my family all will turn back on you wicked. We've done you nothing, but you want to harm us.

Truly good luck to you because in time, you will see and know what is going to happen to you. Your hurt and pain is more than infinitely and indefinitely, more than forever ever guaranteed.

I know what's going to happen to you hence; I fight with no one, and will fight with no one.

Michelle

As for Blacks that are going to come after me for their beloved bible, let me reiterate again.

I WILL NOT FIGHT WITH YOU FOR YOUR BELIEFS OF GARBAGE WHEN IT COMES TO YOUR GOD, AND RELIGION.

BELIEF KILL THE SPIRIT AND SOUL.

RELIGION IS NOT OF GOD

RELIGION IS A LIE

RELIGION IS A WAY FOR MEN, WOMEN, AND CHILDREN TO MAKE MONEY OFF YOU BECAUSE; RELIGION IS A MONEY MAKING INSTITUTION AND OR, ORGANIZATION.

You are the prophet and profit for the wicked and evil of this earth. Yes, the same word but spelt differently, and have the same meaning despite the definition of man, and man's dictionary.

Money that you give these churches do not truly benefit the poor, or the community you live in, nor does it benefit you. You the people are the scapegoat for the different religious leaders of the globe. Therefore, many of you are the prostitutes, and sex slaves of the clergy; your clerical leaders.

God is not about money; I know this for a fact beyond doubt.

God do not deal in money I know this for a fact beyond doubt.

God's true blessing is; **WATER.**

When you ask God to bless you, God bless you with water. Therefore, I will fight with no one for your religious beliefs.

Michelle
February 2019

Family and people; my true family, I dreamt about me feuding with Blacks of old I could not see about religion. I know for a fact religion is truly not of God because; God do not give lies, or dirty things.

Black People; some Black People are too gullible. Readily accept things, and lose their place with God then complain about the shit of crap you accept. Man give dirty hence, many put self above God; good and true life.

If you know a race a people hate your ass; why accept them, and their lies?

Why stay in their abusive system and systems of systemic racism, and oppression?

Unnu mussi love pain and oppression fi real.

Onwards I go

Other Blacks have to defend their religion and god. **RELIGION IS THEIR KEEP, SO THEY HAVE TO DEFEND DEATH.**

Some Blacks do defend DEATH, and will forever defend DEATH because; DEATH IS THEIR GOD, and this is their right.

They have a right to defend their god, and beliefs.

All that is nasty and evil they have to defend because; nastiness is their nature, and nastiness is engrained in their physical, and spiritual DNA. They cannot change this hence; ***HELL IS THEIR TRUE AND NATURAL HOME; DOMAIN.***

Michelle
February 2019

MY WORLD OF DREAMS 2019 – BOOK FOUR

It's Family Day today people. February 18, 2019

Happy Family Day to the true families out there.

Happy Family Day Lovey, and my gorgeous and beautiful mother. May your day, and Lovey's day be bright, happy, and clear.

Many good and true blessings be bestowed on the both of you.

You are both my good and true cheer.

May all the goodness of life and you surround me and my children, these books, you both, my physical and spiritual health, life, finances, wealth, debts, living, and more continually without end in a good and true way.

As I look to the both of you for strength, good health, protection; all my needs and wants, I bestow blessings of truth, prosperity, good health and wealth, and more on the both of you in a good, clean, and true way.

Once again my beloveds; Happy Family Day.

Michelle

Did I dream about Japan, and the English monarchy?

Yes

Dreamt England controlled the land and people hence, the queen, now queen of England controlled the land, and people.

In the dream, the people were not free to make decisions for themselves.

Therefore, I asked this one Japanese lady who had a different eye colour of blue and green; no not green but smoky blue I would say, and iris of black brown if the country was a sovereign nation, and she said no.

Upon hearing that, the queen was upset, and she said something in anger. I cannot tell you what she said. However, **_I needed the land to be sovereign; free of the English Monarch._**

Yes, the people could travel to other lands, and one young looking man was asked to go into another land, but he said no.

Will not analyze this dream because I truly do not know. So I am leaving this dream alone.

Michelle
February 18, 2019

MY WORLD OF DREAMS 2019 – BOOK FOUR

Dreamt I was somewhere. It was like the Caribbean and Canada all in one.

This dream had young; very green and small fruits on this tree.

I would say oranges, but the fruits looked different from tiny and or, baby oranges.

The tree was tall, and full of fruits; green fruits. The tree was also dirty. Like Caribbean dirt was on the tree, and in the air. Caribbean dirty – I cannot explain it any better.

Think dry air and dirt, and vehicles travelling, and dust got on the tree if that makes any sense to you.

This young Black Girl was beside me now, and she was telling me the names of different oranges, as well as; three alcoholics in her town.

She told me their names, but I so can't remember their names.

Also, I can't remember the name of the town.

Bedford just popped in my head, but like I said; it was a Canada Caribbean dream all in one. Two countries in one.

I do not know what the dream mean, and I am so going to leave it at that because I've never dreamt two countries in one before. At least not in this way.

Michelle
February 18, 2019

As for the weather, I cannot tell you of where is going to get hit next weather wise.

It's implied there is going to be weather disasters that has to do with the sea.

Implied dreams I worry not about. ***I truly do not know what implied dreams signify.***

Why did LA, and water – the ocean and or, sea just pop into my head?

Me seeing the water there. Meaning I am seeing water there.

Oh well, I am so not worried because, life here on earth has changed.

Humans are dying because the hearts of men; humans have changed. Have become wicked and vile towards each other.

Altered state, mind, genetic makeup, humans physical makeup chemically – food we eat, and water we drink.

Yes, all comes down to ***MONEY FOR THE CORRUPT, AND EVIL FEW.***

Michelle
February 18, 2019

Jamaica I truly do not care about your politics, and your corrupt, and nasty political leaders there.

They have no morals, or moral values just like you the people. So whatever evil befall the island is rightfully deserved. You the people caused this on self.

You the people elected demons to oversee all of you.

You the people allow your children to listen to the music of demons therefore, allowing demons to infest the island, and the hearts of many of you, and your children.

Nuff a unnu too falla batty. Love fi falla evil to unnu death.

None of you are truly looking into things. Unnu done. Have, and has become the sacrifice for many.

Yes, there is more so however Death kill; take your lives; the life of you Jamaicans, you deserve it because; unnu licky licky and dunkya. Unnu sell out self fi a couple dalla. So don't cry as violence; death escalate on land. Unnu call it dung pan self.

You chose; **_all of you chose DEATH OVER LIFE._** So die.

Death was your choice, and death is claiming. I feel sorry for none of you because; **_you were all SACRIFICED TO DEATH._**

Si di blood sacrifices wey some a di musicians a du fi fame an money. Yes chicken – animal, blood, and human sacrifices.

Dyam fool fool. **_STOP ENTERTAINING THE DEMONS OF HELL._**

Michelle
February 18, 2019

MY WORLD OF DREAMS 2019 – BOOK FOUR

This dream is odd for me because I can make no sense of it.

This young black female that I would say in her late thirties to early forties if not younger.

She was the new leader of this church. She was happy and smiling, and of dark chocolate complexion. Not too dark. She was the leader of this church. She took over as the leader.

There wasn't much people in the church. Three (3) males.

She took to the pulpit area and instead of going into another room to change, she sat at the pulpit and took off her clothes. Then she slid naked like a snake on the pulpit, then sat up.

Opening her legs she put a cloth between her legs for her vagina not to show.

Then this man was telling her about the decline in sales, and radio promotion. Radio promotion was down by a thousand I believe. Overall decline was by thousand, and thousands.

We began to discuss business, and I said; "good clean business cannot decline," and this man agreed with me.

At any rate, the conversation went on. This young man now was talking about his dad. He was going to cry. I think his dad was the owner of the church that the lady I described above took over for. The church was taken from him from the discussion.

His dad's name was Tookie, Twokie, Toukie. Toukie was his father's name; with me giving you the different spellings for Toukie. He said; does anyone have Toukie's number, and an elder that I know in real life but have not seen in years gave him Toukie's number.

The number is: 280 - 9227.

I so do not know what that number represent, or the area code of that number.

Hey, it could be Toukie's time he's going to spend in hell.

If you know let me know.

My email address is: michellejeanbooks@gmail.com.

Michelle
February 18, 2019

Have not been keeping a dream journal everyone.

Oh man, I forgot something when it came to the tree dream I gave you.

In the dream, my language was the way I write. Meaning, how I speak is the way I write.

I was going to send some of my writings out to the Caribbean, but I have to rethink this decision due to cleanliness, and disappointment.

And yes, I am dreaming about the Cayman Islands again. Someone in the government there is selling off the land yet again.

<u>Once again, we as Black People elect corrupt scumbags to lead us. Scumbags that do nothing but line their pocket with blood, and corrupt money. Money they gladly accept, and leave you the people of the land needy, and needing.</u>

Your welfare, and stability means absolutely nothing to them.

They are fed, while others own the island, and you the people of the land own nothing. So once again, I blame you the people of the land that elect the dungs of the earth to oversee, and govern you. Therefore, there are no good governance at the head of you.

As governments lack moral, and moral values; so do the people of the land. And yes, I will be banned from entering

Cayman, and other lands due to what I see, tell you, and write in these books.

Hey, it bothers me not hence, I truly worry not about the different lands of the globe. The corrupt will always live corrupt – thieves that rob the people of their land's prosperity, and wealth.

Michelle
February 18, 2019

This is not my crazy thought, but January 29th I dream Lovey wanted me to fail financially.

Nothing new for me because I knew Lovey could not make me truly happy.

I guess this is my **_FOR THE GOOD TIMES_** moment by **_Al Green_** when it comes to Lovey and me.

It's sad when you put your trust, and all into someone; a being that you thought was true to you, only to find out that someone and or, being want you to fail in life financially.

I know truth cannot fail, and never will fail, yet; Lovey was not truly true to me, and for me. Meaning, Lovey was not my true truth when it comes to his and or, true truth of me.

I will not dwell on this dream, or my loss because; I know tomorrow and time.

Life is truly not about material gain, but it's sad that in the physical realm you cannot be happy financially.

Debt is not nice, and it would be truly nice to be debt free.

I cannot force Lovey to truly love me in everyway, or anyway.

It's his and or, his loss knowing that truth was not within from the get go.

Do not ask someone to write then set them up for failure. Where's the justness in you when you do this?

When you set someone up to fail; you hate them come on now.

Like I said; I am not worried because tomorrow comes, and I am not the one failing Lovey. Lovey is the one failing me.

Michelle
January 29, 2019

MY WORLD OF DREAMS 2019 – BOOK FOUR

It's sad when you trust so truthfully yet, the one you give your all, and trust to cannot be trusted.

When Lovey do this; set you up for failure; it's not you losing your life, but Lovey. Lovey is losing his, and her life.

Truth cannot sin.
Truth cannot fail.

Truth can only be true.

Yes, the spiritual world has, and have changed.

Lovey has, and have changed also.

Lovey has to know his, and her life.

Hell is there; thus hell is the home for billions.

If Lovey want to go to hell and die, then that choice is Lovey's, and Lovey's alone.

Michelle
January 29, 2019

MY WORLD OF DREAMS 2019 – BOOK FOUR

I refuse to worry about why Lovey want me to fail financially.

I refuse to put Lovey's hatred of me in this way on my head.

I am tool old for nonsense. Too old for the unjust way, and ways of Lovey.

I need to worry about me, my health, and life.

If Lovey want, and need someone else to do for him, or her; then so be it. Lovey can go at any time.

All Lovey is telling me right now is that; Lovey was never my forever ever mine; truth, and true truth.

Truth cannot set up anyone for failure.

I will forever ever stay true to me, my truth, and the truth I've come to learn, and know.

Michelle
January 29, 2019

If Lovey want to lose me, that's Lovey's loss, and not mine.

I have to stay true to me.

I have to be the good me I can be.

As long as I am not the false and or, wrong one, I am more than truly good to go.

Listen family and people, I am not the one to be singing ***I MISS YOU*** by Harold Melvin and the Bluenotes. Lovey will be the one.

I'm not the one that is going to be empty; Lovey is the one to be empty.

Lovey will be the one to be crying knowing that I am gone, and never ever coming back.

So yes, I worry not about Lovey setting me up to fail financially.

Trust me, I won't call Lovey to see how Lovey is doing.

Trust me, Lovey will be the one to be hunting me down begging me for forgiveness.

Hey, life isn't about lies. Trust me, I am free.

No more dreams of death; well not so much.

Yea me, freedom. So if Lovey want to go then so be it.

Death won't be around me so much.

I am sleeping better – wait. I am sleeping better.

Yep, happy life.
Happy me.

Truly, truly, truly love me true.

Michelle
January 29, 2019

If you Lovey did not want me to exclude the <u>WHITE RACE based on hue, and based on hue and evil deeds off your Mountain of Goodness and Truth, then you should have said so.</u>

You should not have asked me to write also.

You cannot have people defying life here on earth.

Death is not the answer to life and you know this.

We have to walk good and true in life, and to life.

How can we reach you if we are filled with sin, and living amongst wicked and evil people?

How can you be our way, direct way, direct truth, direct energy, clean source; if we are unclean constantly, and continually?

Lies cannot find you Lovey. Therefore, you cannot be my stairway if lies are involved.

How can I come up to you if my stairway, and your stairway is flawed; is broken on the way?

We need to fix the climate of us, and this earth.

Each individual here on earth have to fix their climate of self come on now.

So truly think Lovey. If you need this to be our final goodbye; say so instead of setting me up for failure financially.

Michelle
January 29, 2019

It's amazing how I cannot find any mercy in you Lovey because you protect the merciless.

How can you want someone; me to fail?

Have you no heart; true heart when it comes to truth, true love, the truth, and absolute truth of life?

What do you gain when you fail yourself; fail your own chosen; the ones you have chosen to write; tell the truth, cure and or, heal for you?

What does it profit, and prophet you to turn against your good and true own in the end?

Therefore, Satan is not the only deceitful one in all of this. You are deceitful also.

You are a liar also.

Truth cannot lie I know, but were you ever truthful, and truly truthful to me?

When you set up someone for failure, are you not spiteful when it comes to that person?

Do you not hate that person?

So now tell me; if you as God, Good God and Allelujah cannot be trusted, how can we as humans trust you, trust our self, and trust others?

Wow

It's amazing how we quarrel. We were going so fine now to have this; me fussing with you, and drawing out your negatives.

No, don't smile because something is truly wrong with you hence, the spiritual realm for 2019 has, and have changed. I truly do not know what to expect life wise anymore.

Michelle
January 29, 2019

No, I cannot fully, and truly go ballistic on you Lovey anger wise due to my dream of you wanting me to fail financially.

On this day, I refuse to because I know my financial worth; prosperity was taken from me long ago, and you've done absolutely nothing of significance to change this.

Know this Lovey:

My life, health, spirit, finances are, and is truly valuable, and important to me.

My physical and spiritual travels is, and are truly valuable, and important to me.

My physical and spiritual well being is, and are valuable, and important to me.

All of me is, and are valuable, and important to me.

All good and true life is, and are important, and valuable to me.

All that is good and true to me that's in my life is, and are valuable, and important to me.

Yes, you Lovey despite my dream, you are and is, valuable, and important to me.

I cannot deny my truth in life.

I cannot deny my place, and space with you in life either.

Yes, it's a shame my dream world had to show me what it did, but what else is new?

Show me something I truly do not, or did not know.

Now the question I ask you is; **why do you want me to fail financially?**

How do I fail financially with you Lovey when *WATER* is your true wealth, stay, place, blessing, and blessings?

Your true worth and wealth is truly not physical, but spiritual thus life; the good and true life that you give.

Wow

The spiritual realm truly need to be cleaned up Lovey.

True love always.

Michelle
January 30, 2019

MY WORLD OF DREAMS 2019 – BOOK FOUR

It's February 25, 2019, and I am going to end this book.

I did dream Tarrus Riley. He did not speak. He was just looking. He looked like the picture on his Love Contagious album. I will not speculate on this dream because, I do not know what silence in my dream world represent.

I so cannot remember my dreams because they were all over the place.

Me being back in time; the 18 hundreds and or, earlier in time.

Me singing a new song.

Destruction and or, devastation that I am being shielded from seeing.

I am so not going to worry about anything. I know I have to get out of North America.

So as I close this book, I dedicate **_NEVER GIVE UP MY PRIDE_** by the reggae artist Luciano to Lovey for Lovey to know that; I will never ever give up my place, and stay in life; good and true life for anyone. I was, and still is made right, and I am going to continue to walk, write, talk, travel, sleep, and be right. I know the spiritual realm is against me, but I truly do not give a damn. **_I KNOW LOVEY, AND THE WEALTH OF LOVEY._** So no matter what they try, and how they in the spiritual world try for me to deceive, and give up Lovey I cannot.

Lovey has no financial spiritual wealth; money family and people; my true family. **_Lovey's financial wealth is water,_** and this is why water is so abundant here on earth, in our body in the form of blood, in the spiritual realm, the universe, and on the moon in the form of ice.

So yes; I know, and cannot believe.

Oh Allelujah, Lovey have mercy on my soul. It's 2:47 pm February 25, 2019 and why did I just see a White Man with his hand open standing above the water/sea?

I also dreamt Butch Stewart, the owner of the Sandals hotel chain a while back. He was sitting in a crowd of people as if they were honouring others.

Michelle
February 25, 2019

BOOKS WRITTEN BY MICHELLE JEAN 2019

MY WORLD OF DREAMS 2019 – BOOK ONE

MY WORLD OF DREAMS 2019 – BOOK TWO

MY WORLD OF DREAMS 2019 – BOOK THREE